PICTURE *of* LOVE

MARRIAGE PREPARATION PROGRAM FOR CONVALIDATION COUPLES

Participant's Workbook

Revised Edition

PICTURE *of* LOVE

MARRIAGE PREPARATION
PROGRAM FOR
CONVALIDATION COUPLES

Participant's Workbook

Revised Edition

by

Joan Vienna, M.A.

Virginia Metoyer, M.A.

CHURCH
PUBLISHING
INCORPORATED

The *Nihil Obstat* and *Imprimatur* are official declarations that the work contains nothing contrary to Faith and Morals. It is not implied thereby that those granting the *Nihil Obstat* and *Imprimatur* agree with the contents, statements, or opinions expressed.

NIHIL OBSTAT: Fr. Michael J. Barrett, S.T.D.
                 Censor Deputatus
IMPRIMATUR: ✠ His Excellency, Most Reverend José H. Gomez
                 Archbishop of Los Angeles
DATE: 6 February 2017

Church Publishing Incorporated
Editorial Offices
19 East 34th Street
New York, NY 10016

Cover Photo: Studio Zanello/Streetstock Images
Photos: Pages 8, 38: jeffjaq; page 10: Wavebreakmedia Ltd; pages 12, 31: monkeybusinessimages; page 14: dolgachov; page 17: g-stockstudio: page 20: Deklofenak; page 28: pixelheadphoto; page 35: Jose Luis Pelaez Inc

Printed in the United States of America

ISBN-13: 978-1-60674-320-1

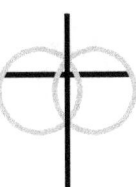

Table of Contents

Welcome to Marriage Preparation 7

Candle Ceremony 8

Sacrament of Matrimony 10

Your Family of Origin 12

Couple Communication 14

Conflict Resolution 17

Finances 20

Married Intimacy 28

Parenting in Today's World 31

Spirituality: Bringing It Home 35

Prayers 38

Additional Topics for Reflection and Discussion

Ecumenical and Interfaith Couples 41

Natural Family Planning 43

Your Family/My Family, They're *Our* Family Now! 47

QuickWrites 50

Agree/Disagree 51

Marriage Preparation Evaluation Form 53

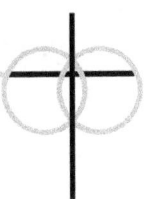

Welcome to Marriage Preparation

Welcome to the *Picture of Love Marriage Preparation Program*. Congratulations on your decision to rededicate your lives to God by becoming a sacramental couple.

Your marriage is cherished by the people of the Catholic Church. You are the hope and future of the Church. We look to your love and enthusiasm for each other to renew and inspire the life of the Church. Your uniqueness as a couple makes you a wonderful gift, and your love for one another will draw others to want to be part of your faith community.

The Catholic Church wants to support you in your times of challenge and struggle and rejoice with you in your times of joy and celebration. We believe in your love for one another, and we are overjoyed that you have chosen to share your sacrament with us.

Picture of Love was created to help you gain a better understanding of the joys and challenges of living the sacrament of Matrimony in your day-to-day lives. It offers you the opportunity to focus on your pictures of marriage. These pictures include your dreams, expectations, and ideas about your upcoming marriage in the Church. The secret is to be able to share these images with each other in order to build better understanding and support for one another.

The marriage preparation team couple's gift to you is to paint a picture of the sacrament of Matrimony. They do this by sharing with you both the intimate and loving moments and the trials and tribulations of married life. Each team presentation, informative enrichment, and couple's exercise is designed to help you gain insights into your relationship as well as give you practical ideas and tools to help smooth your journey and become the *Picture of Love* to one another.

We thank all the priests and couples who have shared so generously their ideas and experience. They are truly an ongoing "picture of love" and living sign of the sacrament of Matrimony.

We dedicate this book to our most ardent supporters, our husbands Anthony Vienna and Paul Metoyer.

May God bless you today and forever.

Mrs. Joan Vienna, M.A.
Mrs. Virginia (Candy) Metoyer, M.A.

Candle Ceremony

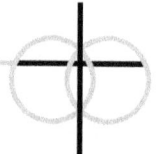

The leader begins by saying:

- As we begin, we light this candle as a reminder that your love for one another is a sign of the presence of God's love in the world.
- Please join us in the following ceremony.

A couple is invited to light the candle together.

Couples together pray:
Lord, as we are about to be married in the Catholic Church,
    help us to prepare with zeal, hope, and enthusiasm
    for our wedding day.
May our efforts be a reminder—today and always—
    that we are called to be your light in the world.
With your grace
    may we grow together in understanding and respect,
    offering to one another our unconditional love and
    life-long commitment.
With your forgiveness
    may we learn to let go of past hurts and resentments
    and to reconcile and heal with one another.

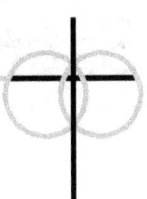

With your loving presence
  may we become a stronger couple and role model
  for our family, friends, and others who journey with us through this life.
Strengthen us with your sacramental graces
  as we invite you to be with us today and always.
Through Christ, Our Lord.
  Amen.

After the reading of Scripture, the leader invites all to pray the Lord's Prayer together:

Our Father, who art in heaven,
hallowed be thy name;
thy kingdom come,
thy will be done
on earth as it is in heaven.
Give us this day our daily bread,
and forgive us our trespasses,
as we forgive those who trespass against us;
and lead us not into temptation,
but deliver us from evil.
Amen.

Sacrament of Matrimony

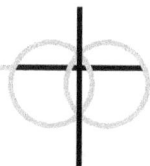

In *The Joy of Love*, Pope Francis teaches married couples that "their union is real and irrevocable, confirmed and consecrated by the sacrament of Matrimony. Yet in joining their lives, the spouses assume an active and creative role in a lifelong project. Their gaze now has to be directed to the future that, with the help of God's grace, they are daily called to build. For this very reason, neither spouse can expect the other to be perfect. Each must set aside all illusions and accept the other as he or she actually is: an unfinished product, needing to grow, a work in progress" (Post-Synodal Apostolic Exhortation *Amoris Lætitia*, Chapter 218).

Becoming the Living Sign of God's Love

The esteem in which the Catholic Church holds the sacrament of Matrimony is reflected in the fact that the couple does not just *receive* this sacrament, they *become* the sacrament. The bride and groom bind themselves in sacred trust—each to the other—with the priest as the witness. Christ so believed in the couple's love for each other that he chose it to be a sign of his love to the world.

By choosing to marry in the Catholic Church, you make a conscious decision to partner with God as your source of strength. Take this decision seriously—you are choosing to make a lifelong covenant with each other and with God!

Your decision to be married in the Catholic Church means:

- You are freely coming to the Church.
- You promise permanence and fidelity to each other.
- You accept children in your life.
- You want more than a civil ceremony.
- You want God to be an essential part of your relationship.
- God calls you to share your sacrament with others as a sign of Christ's love to the world.
- Sanctifying graces flow from your sacramental relationship that strengthen you and guide you on your journey.

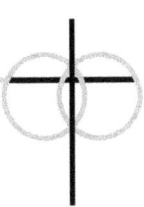

Reflection Questions

- I want to be married in the Catholic Church because ... *(Check all that apply.)*

  ☐ I want to live out God's plan for us as a couple.

  ☐ I want to go to communion.

  ☐ I want to fix our marriage.

  ☐ of family pressure.

  ☐ of pressure from my spouse.

  ☐ *(Other?)* _____.

- In what ways can you share your sacrament with others? *(Check all that apply.)*

  ☐ Go to church each Sunday.

  ☐ Volunteer to help the parish.

  ☐ Reflect our love for each other by respecting each other.

  ☐ Raising children to love God.

  ☐ *(Other?)* _____.

- Circle the word that best describes your feelings about attending this program:

Excited	Anxious	Proud	Comfortable
Upset	Frustrated	Worried	Hopeful

  (Other?) _____

For Ecumenical or Interfaith Couples

Note: Be sure to read Ecumenical and Interfaith Couples found on pages 41–42 at the back of this *Workbook.*

As you each honor your own faith expression, what do you see as the challenges to your relationship in living out your sacred union?

_____

_____

_____

_____

> Every day...
>
> pray for each other;
>
> bless each other;
>
> help each other get to heaven.

Your Family of Origin

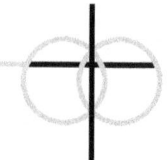

Learning from Your Family of Origin

Your "family of origin," the family in which you were raised, profoundly influences you throughout your lifetime. Here is where you form the image or "picture" of how life should be and how a married couple and family should behave. Your family of origin not only gave you your role models for marriage and family life, they also taught important lessons about values, traditions, attitudes, communications styles, expectations, etc.

Some of you were raised in homes with two parents, others by a single parent, and still others by grandparents or other extended family. Some of you may have experienced being raised in a divorced family and will need to find a new role model for marriage. Some of you enjoyed the positive experience of love, support, stability, and/or faith, while some may have endured negative experience such as abandonment, anger, violence, addiction, and abuse. Or many of you might have experienced a combination of both positive and negative experiences.

This is your opportunity to step back and reflect on your own families of origin and how you want to work together to form your new family. Here is an example of differences that might be experienced:

Nuclear Family

Mother/Father
Catholic
Oldest Child/Daughter
Quiet, Reserved
College Educated
High Expectations

Single-Parent Family

Mother
Protestant
Only Child/Son
Outgoing, Communicative
College Educated
Medium Expectations

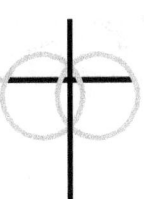

 # Illustrating Your Family of Origin

Draw a picture of your family of origin, including your parents/guardians, siblings, and closest extended family.

The point of understanding your family of origin is to realize that you have choices both as individuals and as a couple. Finding and embracing the positive patterns and behaviors while leaving behind the negative ones enables you to choose how you will handle the joys and stresses of marriage and family life, and to avoid reacting involuntarily with learned responses.

Reflect on the picture you have just drawn.

- On the suitcase below, write two positive patterns or behaviors that you want to bring to your marriage from your family of origin.
- Label the box with the one pattern or behavior you most want to leave behind.

 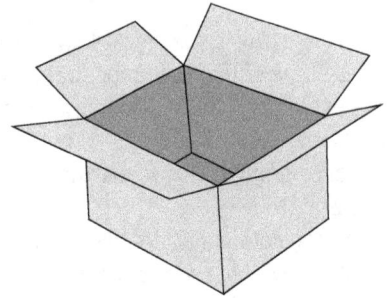

Today is a new beginning for your journey as a couple. Work together throughout your marriage to consciously reflect on and evaluate what you have learned from your family of origin and to choose whether you want those patterns and behaviors to be a part of your marriage and family life. This exercise will help you to build a strong and united marriage.

Couple Communication

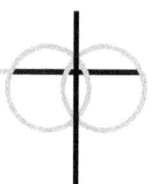

Tips for Constructive Communication

Most couples agree that to have a good marriage, you must communicate. But couples are often unaware of *how* to communicate effectively. Great communication is not just talking to each other, it is a learned skill that takes *information*, *tools*, and *practice*.

The following tips will help you:

- *Careful Listening:* Listening closely to one another is one of the most important building blocks of communication. Good listening requires that you pay attention to both:
  - verbal communication (the actual words being said).
  - nonverbal communication (body language, facial expression, eye contact, etc.).
- *Mutual Respect:* Strive to appreciate and value the other person's personality style, opinions, feelings, values, and beliefs even if they differ from your own. You can nurture mutual respect by:
  - sharing honestly.
  - practicing conflict resolution.

- *Willingness to Focus:* Focusing your full attention on each other will make your communication a constructive and life-giving experience. Doing so requires:
  - quality time devoted to just the two of you.
  - unplugging from distractions (TV, cell phones, other digital devices, etc.).
- *Sharing Perceptions:* Sharing how you view and perceive your world helps couples realize that they are individuals with their own way of viewing situations, experiences, people, events, etc. Working together to understand each other's perceptions is an important building block to communication. To do this you need to:
  - be open to listening to your spouse's thoughts and feelings without judgment.
  - respect each other's differences.
- *Always Remember:* Your spouse is your best friend.

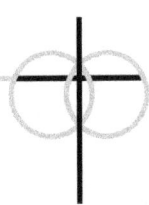

Your Communication Profile

Family of Origin is the first place you learned to communicate. Check the styles of communication you learned as a child:

☐ Noisy	☐ Quiet	☐ Seldom	☐ Constructive
☐ Unwilling	☐ Easy	☐ Fair	☐ Emotional
☐ Abusive	☐ Honest	☐ Kind	☐ Open
☐ Calm	☐ Productive	☐ Other: _____	

Are there any you would like to eliminate?

☐ Yes   ☐ No

Explain:

_____

_____

_____

When you are with your spouse's family, do you find any challenges in the way his or her family communicates compared to your family (for example, outgoing vs. quiet; constructively vs. abusively; etc.)?   ☐ Yes   ☐ No

Give an example:

_____

_____

_____

Personality Characteristics

Each person has certain personality characteristics that affect the way he or she communicates. Check the following characteristics that apply to you, and then do the same for your spouse:

_____ You _____		_____ Your Spouse _____	
☐ Extroverted	☐ Introverted	☐ Extroverted	☐ Introverted
☐ Good listener	☐ Poor listener	☐ Good listener	☐ Poor listener
☐ Needs time to think	☐ Responds quickly	☐ Needs time to think	☐ Responds quickly
☐ Morning person	☐ Night person	☐ Morning person	☐ Night person
☐ Avoids conflict	☐ Confronts conflict	☐ Avoids conflict	☐ Confronts conflict
☐ Talkative	☐ Slow to speak	☐ Talkative	☐ Slow to speak

What is the one personality characteristic that most impacts your communication? In what ways?

_____

_____

_____

_____

Effect of Technology on Communication

Technology, especially social media, has become the dominant way that most people communicate today. Often, spouses are more interested in checking their phones every few minutes than in engaging in meaningful conversation with each other (or their children). The use of technology and social media can be a useful tool, but it can also be a major distraction.

What technology and social media do you use?

_____

_____

_____

_____

How much uninterrupted, face-to-face communication do you have with your spouse each day?

_____

_____

_____

_____

Conflict Resolution

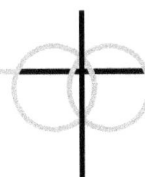

In every couple's relationship, there are bound to be conflicts from time to time. Differences in the ways you were raised, your personalities, expectations, values, etc., make you unique human beings. These differences may also cause problems. Conflict does not mean that you have stopped loving each other; it is a normal part of working out the differences in a marriage. Don't be afraid to fight for your relationship—but learn to fight fair! Here are techniques that may help you.

Ten Techniques for Resolving Conflict

1. Stop. Ask God for Guidance

When you sense the start of conflict, *pause. Pray.* Ask God to direct your thinking, your words, and your actions as you work through the issue.

2. Identify the Issue

This is a critical point. To be able to resolve issues and grow in your relationship, you must know what you are disagreeing about. Sometimes what starts the conflict is not the real issue that requires attention. Consequently, your disagreements can often be confusing and counterproductive.

3. Stick to the Issue

Once you have decided what the issue is, stick to it and do not change the subject. Explore and share your thoughts and feelings about the issue so that you clearly understand each other's perspective and perception. It would not be an issue if one or both of you did not have strong feelings about the issue.

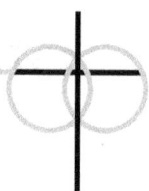

4. Actively Listen to the Other Person Without Interrupting

One of the hardest things to do during a disagreement is to stop and listen to what the other person is trying to say. Often, couples argue to win a point instead of trying to gain understanding. Mutual respect for each other's thoughts and feelings leads to growth and deeper understanding.

5. Use "I" Statements Instead of "You" Statements

"You" statements are instant button-pushers. Statements such as "You never..." or "You always..." send a message that says "I am accusing you or blaming you." Instead, express your concerns in terms of "I want...," "I think...," "I need...," "I feel...." For example, saying, "You are always texting. You care more about others than you do about me," is different from saying, "I am really feeling lonely. Can we take some time just for the two of us without interruptions?"

6. Stay Physically Close

Good eye contact is a critical part of communication. The nonverbal cues can be just as important as the verbal. A picture is worth a thousand words, and many times, paying close attention to the other's nonverbal signals communicates something beyond their words.

7. Don't Bring Up Past History

Past history is just that, *past!* It is not helpful to keep a record of every mistake or hurt. We cannot change yesterday; we can only learn from the experiences. Talking about the present keeps you focused on the current issue.

8. Avoid Involving Third Parties

Leave friends and relatives out of your conflict. They can only complicate the issue, and it puts them in an uncomfortable position. If you need outside help, seek it from a professional therapist.

9. Avoid Criticism

Criticism and sarcasm kill a person's spirit and can damage or destroy the relationship.

10. Finish the Argument

Bring resolution to your arguments. Sometimes, it will mean that you need to change a behavior pattern in your relationship. At other times, it may mean that you agree to disagree. Whatever you do, pledge to one another to complete the argument, even if you can't finish it right then—set a specific time to finish. Carrying a grudge or simply ignoring the conflict allows resentment to grow.

An Important Word about Anger

Patterns of anger and abuse are often learned from the family of origin and may be thought of as normal in a relationship, but they are neither normal nor healthy. Keep the following in mind:

- If at any time during an argument you feel that the level of anger is becoming too high, stop and take an adequate time out to cool off.
- Abuse is *never appropriate* and includes creating fear by trying to control the other person with methods such as bullying, yelling, breaking things, physical violence, and verbal and/or psychological abuse.
- These patterns of behavior are *not* acceptable and can do irreparable harm and damage to the relationship.

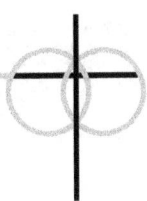

Danger Signs in Your Relationship

Are you...

- afraid to speak to your spouse for fear of his or her anger?
- keeping feelings and thoughts to yourself to keep the peace?
- hiding money, friends, purchases, religious practices, food, liquor, drugs?
- frequently feeling hurt and misunderstood?
- feeling excited to see someone of the opposite sex at work, the gym, or elsewhere?
- feeling as if you want to run away?

- sharing your thoughts and feelings with someone else more easily than with your spouse?
- constantly needing to look for relief from everyday life?

If there is a problem in any of these areas, or if you have experienced physical or emotional abuse in your life, seek professional therapy. Don't allow these destructive patterns into your relationship.

Finances

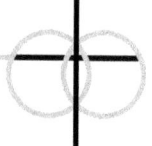

Opening Exercise

1. Who handles the money in your family?

   _____

   _____

2. How many credit cards do you and your spouse have?

   _____

   _____

3. How comfortable are you with the amount of credit debt you owe (individually and as a couple)?

   _____

   _____

4. Do you share all information about accounts (checking, saving, credit, investments) with each other?

   _____

   _____

5. Do you share passwords and access to all of your accounts?

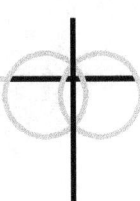

 # Your Financial Profile

1. What does having money mean... (Prioritize on a scale from 1 to 7, with 1 as the highest priority.)

To You

___ Security   ___ Status   ___ Comfort   ___ Freedom

___ Control   ___ Acceptance   ___ Happiness

To Your Spouse

___ Security   ___ Status   ___ Comfort   ___ Freedom

___ Control   ___ Acceptance   ___ Happiness

2. Do you agree or disagree with the following?

	Agree	*Disagree*
Having a monthly budget is important.	____	____
I think we both use credit cards wisely.	____	____
I am comfortable with the financial decisions we have made so far.	____	____
We should have separate checking accounts.	____	____
Our present work situation is acceptable to me.	____	____
We are financially comfortable and satisfied.	____	____

3. What is your most challenging financial concern at this time?

_____

_____

_____

_____

Group Sharing

After reading your assigned scenario, discuss possible solutions for the couple.

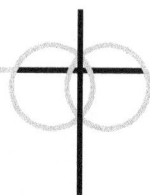

Financial Scenario 1

Mario and Emma have been married for 4 years, and are both employed full time. Emma, a civil engineer for the city, uses her health insurance benefits for the family because her contribution is very reasonable. Mario is a freelance computer contractor with no healthcare benefits. Emma and Mario have just purchased their first home and have two vehicles, one of which has a monthly payment. They have minimum credit card debt and a small student loan that will be paid off in 2 years.

Mario and Emma just had a baby 2 months ago, and Emma is breastfeeding. Emma had arranged to be off from work for 3 months. As the time is approaching for her to return to work, she is unable to find a childcare provider with whom she feels comfortable. Of the two that she has considered, one is in a home setting with five other children and the other is part of a childcare group that runs a chain of facilities with many children. She did not know how difficult it would be to leave her baby in another's care. She really wants to stay home an additional 9 months and continue to care for her baby. She is just not sure that they can manage financially.

Although Mario has been successful in his business and has several signed contracts that will provide a good income for them for the next 6 months, the couple's budget and house payment are based on two incomes. Mario also worries about how they would afford healthcare for themselves and their baby on their own. He would really like to see Emma go back to work as they had planned.

Questions for Group Discussion

- To what extent do you think Emma is being realistic about wanting to stay home with their baby instead of returning to work as planned?
- To what extent do you think Mario is being overly concerned about their financial future?
- What do you feel would be their best option? What advice would you give them?

Financial Scenario 2

Sonia and Malcolm have been married for 2 years. They have decided to look into purchasing a home. Malcolm is an accountant and has worked for a company for 12 years. The company treats its employees well and pays a generous salary based on industry standards. Sonia is a teacher with a public institution and has been teaching for 10 years. They each have good benefits.

Since they married, they have each put money into the joint household account to pay for monthly expenses such as rent and utilities. They also have continued to maintain separate bank accounts and credit cards, which they manage individually. They are now jointly applying to be preapproved for a home loan, which has revealed many things about Sonia's credit that Malcom was unaware of until this point: she has high credit card debt with multiple cards, some late payments, and multiple student loans totaling $65,000. Her low credit score will likely affect their ability to purchase a home.

Questions for Group Discussion

- To what extent do you think Malcolm has a reason to be upset by the situation?
- To what degree do you think this is a joint problem for Malcolm and Sonia? What might Malcolm's responsibility be to help Sonia pay off her debt?
- What other options do Malcolm and Sonia have regarding the purchase of a home?

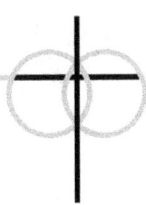

Financial Scenario 3

Adrian and Blanca have been married for 20 years. Adrian has been a high school teacher for the public school system for 25 years and has a good salary and health and other benefits. Blanca is a computer programmer for a small tech company where she has worked for the last 12 years and has a decent salary but no benefits. Adrian and Blanca have three children ages 18, 15, and 10, all in public school. They are buying their home and have a reasonable monthly payment along with two cars, one that is 3 years old (with a payment) and one that is 11 years old (that is paid off). Adrian and Blanca have credit card debt on three cards for a total of $20,000. Adrian just finished his master's degree, so he also has a student loan for $25,000, and their son will graduate from high school in 7 months and would like to be able to go away to school.

Financially, they are relatively secure right now, but they can see a lot of expenses coming up in the near future. Added to all of her family expenses, Blanca knows that her parents are counting on them to contribute money to them every month to meet their monthly expenses now that they can no longer work and their health is declining. Her parents provided this same type of assistance for both sets of their parents, and Blanca knows they are looking to her and her sister for help.

Blanca is really worried that Adrian will not consent to this expense because he is worried about paying off their credit card debt, his student loan, and their son's educational expenses. They will also need a new car in a few years. Blanca doesn't know what to do because she doesn't want to let her parents down, but she also knows that she and Adrian are stretched pretty thin financially.

Questions for Group Discussion

- What advice would you give to Adrian and Blanca regarding agreeing to contribute monthly to her parent's expenses?
- Should Blanca give her parents money without telling Adrian?
- Do Blanca's parents have the right to assume that Blanca and Adrian will help them financially?

After the discussion, take a few minutes quietly to consider your relationship with your spouse. If you have any concerns about your finances, be sure to communicate them to your spouse. If you encounter difficulties you cannot resolve together, discuss the possibility of seeking professional financial counseling.

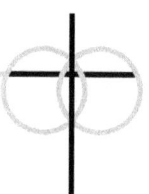

Sample Budget Sheet

In the spaces provided, place the dollar amount that you, as a couple, currently spend or budget on each of the items.

Monthly Income

His _____   Hers _____   Other _____   **Total** _____

Housing

Rent/Mortgage _____
Utilities _____
Home Repair _____
Phone _____
Internet/Cable _____
Total _____

Auto

Payments _____
Gasoline _____
Insurance _____
Repairs _____
Other _____
Total _____

Groceries

Food _____
Medicine _____
Toiletries _____
Paper goods _____
Other _____
Total _____

Personal

Clothes _____
Gifts _____
Dry Cleaning _____
Salon/Barber _____
Total _____

Recreation

Dining Out _____
Movies, etc. _____
Vacations _____
Pets _____
Total _____

Debt

Credit Card _____
Student Loan _____
Personal Loan _____
Other _____
Total _____

Education

Tuition _____
Books _____
Fees _____
Other _____
Total _____

Medical

Insurance Premium _____
Prescriptions _____
Dental/Doctor _____
Copays _____
Total _____

Contribution

Church _____
Charities _____
Family _____
Other _____
Total _____

Savings

Savings _____
Investments _____
Retirement _____
Total _____

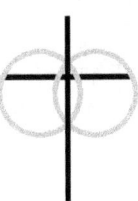

Total Monthly Expenses and Income

Enter the total from each of the categories on page 24.

Housing	_____
Personal	_____
Education	_____
Auto	_____
Recreation	_____
Medical	_____
Groceries	_____
Debt	_____
Contributions	_____
Savings	_____
Total Expenses	_____

Subtract your total monthly expenses from your total monthly income.

Total Income	_____
Total Expenses	_____
Positive Balance	_____

or

Negative Balance (_____)

After subtracting your total monthly expenses from your total monthly income, you will have either a positive or negative balance.

- If the balance is positive on an ongoing basis—and you have some savings as a cushion—you are headed in the right direction.
- If the balance is negative, you will need to increase your income or decrease your expenses. By doing so, you decrease your chances of being in debt.

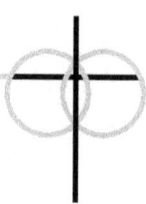

Adding Children to Your Budget

You can expand the Sample Budget Sheet into a family budget by considering the following:

- What insurance plans do we have in place? Do they cover childbirth?
- Do we have paid family leave as part of our benefits? If so, for how long?
- What are the benefits and costs of one of us staying home versus using childcare?
- What is our medical coverage for additional family members?
- What will be our additional cost for items such as baby food, diapers, clothing, crib, etc.?
- How will we plan for the extra costs of preschool, Catholic education, and so on?

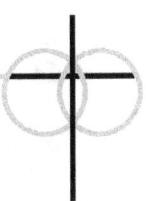

The High Cost of Debt

Debt costs you money. People are often unaware of the high price they pay for the use of credit cards, house loans, car loans, and similar debt.

Credit Card Debt: What Is the Best Way to Pay?

As an example, let's imagine you have a credit card with a *$2000 balance at 15% interest.* Here is what happens under three different payment options:

Option 1: You Make the Minimum Payment Each Month

With this plan, you would expect to pay about $44 a month in the beginning. However, as your balance decreases, so does the minimum payment, so you pay less of the balance each month, which substantially increases the interest you pay over the time period. In fact, it will take you *17 years* to pay off your credit card, and you can expect to pay *$1929 in interest,* which is only $71 less than the original balance of $2000. That almost doubles the purchase price!

Option 2: You Make a Constant Payment Each Month

If you choose to continue paying the $44 every month until the credit card is paid off (even though it's no longer the required minimum payment), it will only take you *5 years and 6 months* to pay off the credit card. You will pay about *$872* in interest.

Option 3: You Make a Constant Payment Each Month, Twice the Original Minimum Payment

If you double your payment to $88 a month (which is double the constant payment), it will take you about *2 years and 3 months* to pay it off. You will pay about *$339* in interest.

Time and interest will vary with different credit card companies. You can see, however, just how much credit card debt can cost. This is just *one* credit card—imagine if you are paying interest on multiple cards!

What can you do?

- Whenever possible, pay off credit card balances each month.
- If you do need to use credit, make educated choices based on your credit options.
- Seek the advice of a certified financial counselor. A financial counselor can help you determine the best financial plan.

Married Intimacy

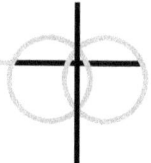

The Cycle of Romance, Disillusionment, and True Joy

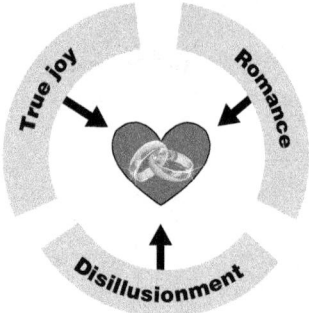

No matter how intimate a couple is, they still go through the cycle of romance, disillusionment, and true joy in their day-to-day lives. A couple goes through this cycle over and over, sometimes more than once a day. This is a natural pattern in any relationship but especially in marital relationships.

Romance

When you are in this stage, you feel happy, lighthearted, and content. Little annoyances are overlooked, and faults go unnoticed.

Disillusionment

This is a time when you feel lonely, hurt, and defensive. You hold back from communicating, which pulls you apart. You can get stuck in this stage by insisting on making your own feelings and needs number one.

True Joy

This stage is characterized by feelings of trust, unity, and love. By making the daily decision to love, you can create an atmosphere in which it is easy to share, love, and grow. Keeping each other and your relationship number one leads to true joy.

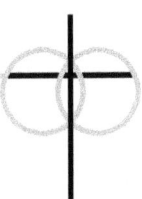

The Key to Intimacy: "Love Is a Decision" (*adapted from the Marriage Encounter Weekend*)

Love is not merely a feeling. Feelings can come and go; for this reason, there are times you may not feel like being loving. At such times, you can call on the sanctifying graces that you received through the sacrament of Matrimony to help you to make a conscious decision to love. As you work through the stages of romance, disillusionment, and true joy, you continue to grow as a couple.

Defining Intimacy

In every aspect of their relationship, the degree of respect, openness, and mutual love with which a husband and wife treat each other affects the depth of their intimacy. God gives married couples the gift of sex as the ultimate physical expression of their love for one another and a reflection of their everyday intimacy.

1. Identify couples you view as being intimate. What are the special qualities of their relationship that made you choose them?

   Intimate Couples I Know   Their Special Qualities

   _____

   _____

   _____

   _____

2. Do you think of yourselves as an intimate couple?

   ____ Yes   ____ No

Intimacy Busters

Any of the following items, when used in excess, can become "intimacy busters" that invade your time and closeness as a couple. Check any of the items that are affecting your relationship:

☐ Reading	☐ Television	☐ Internet	☐ Gaming	☐ Cell Phone
☐ Excessive Exercise	☐ Career	☐ Tiredness	☐ School	☐ Friends
☐ Family	☐ Social Networking	☐ Sports	☐ Hobbies	☐ Sleep

Other _____

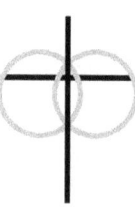

3. How do the above "Intimacy Busters" affect the time you spend together and your closeness as a couple?

_____

_____

_____

_____

AAAs of Intimacy

By practicing these AAAs of Intimacy, you can nurture your decision to love:

- *Attention:* Take quality time each day to focus on one another without distractions. Let each other know he or she is worthy of your full attention. Make a promise to "unplug" once a week for a few hours from all technology and electronics and just be together.
- *Affection:* Show each other tenderness both verbally and physically. Express your love each day.
- *Appreciation:* Verbally affirm with praise and encouragement. Say how much you appreciate and respect each other. Always be thankful for the gift you are to one another.

If you practice the AAAs every day, you will always be life-giving to one another. Being life-giving means doing or saying that which nurtures your spouse's spirit, that which builds each other up and helps the two of you on your journey to heaven.

4. What is your favorite way for your spouse to show you he or she loves you?

_____

_____

_____

_____

Parenting in Today's World

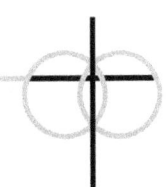

Part 1

For Couples with a Child or Children

Read each of the following statements and check *Agree* if you think the statement is correct or *Disagree* if you think the statement is incorrect. The presenting team will tell you when it is time to compare your answers and complete Part 2.

Agree	Disagree	
☐	☐	1. Negative patterns of parenting in my/your family of origin may be affecting our family today.
☐	☐	2. I like the parenting styles that we have each developed with our children.
☐	☐	3. I think the way we share responsibility for the care of our child/children is fair.
☐	☐	4. I am comfortable with how we discipline our child/children.
☐	☐	5. I think we both spend enough time with our child/children.

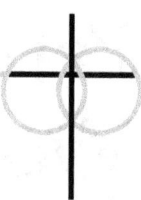

Agree	Disagree	
☐	☐	6. We communicate well in the area of parenting.
☐	☐	7. I experience our child/children dividing us at times.
☐	☐	8. I am comfortable with my parents and/or my spouse's parents giving us advice about parenting.
☐	☐	9. I think that we are good parents.
☐	☐	10. The quality of our marriage directly affects the lives of our children.

For Couples without Children

Read each of the following statements and check *Agree* if you think the statement is correct or *Disagree* if you think the statement is incorrect. The presenting team will tell you when it is time to compare your answers and complete Part 2.

Agree	Disagree	
☐	☐	1. We agree on when we want to start our family and how many children we want to have.
☐	☐	2. I am excited about the idea of us becoming parents.
☐	☐	3. I like the role models for parenting that my/your family of origin has given us.
☐	☐	4. There are some negative patterns of parenting from my/your family of origin that I want to discard.
☐	☐	5. I think it is important for each of us to have our separate time alone after we have children.
☐	☐	6. We will take turns getting up at night and caring for our baby.
☐	☐	7. One parent should stay home to raise the child/children during the formative years.
☐	☐	8. We should always take the baby with us when we go out.
☐	☐	9. I have some fears or doubts about being a parent.
☐	☐	10. Our communication patterns will change after we have a baby.

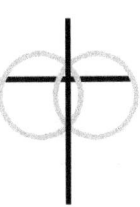

Part 2

After hearing the presentation and comparing your answers with your spouse, what area of parenting do you need to discuss?

_____

_____

_____

_____

Family Decision Making

In your time together, you have made many decisions, some small and others big. Some were easy to make, especially when you both agreed on the decision or neither had a strong opposing feeling. At other times, it may have been more difficult. Varying needs, wants, feelings, and expectations can deeply affect your decision making.

Many decisions revolve around family. For example:

- What do we each believe should be the size of our family?
- Are we satisfied with our childcare arrangements? Are we content with the size of our home and our neighborhood? Who will discipline the children? Do we agree on how we are disciplining our children.
- Is my/our relationship with my/your in-laws going well?

Ongoing communication about decision making is critical, both to you as a couple and to you as a family. Teaching children how to make constructive decisions is an important part of parenting. When your children see you working through a decision together, they are given an important role model. When they are allowed, with your guidance, to make decisions for themselves and with the family, they learn skills that they can use throughout their lives.

Six Steps of Decision Making

1. _Pray Together:_ Pray together about important decisions so you will be God-centered. What values are important to each of you? Would the decision support your values?

2. _Discern:_ Gather the facts. Read information that is available on the subject. Ask someone who is knowledgeable about the issue under consideration for their opinion, but not just those who will support your point of view.

3. _Identify Pros and Cons:_ Make a separate list of the pros and cons that each of you see regarding the decision you are trying to make. Share these lists with each other. Make a final list together that you can work from to make your decision.

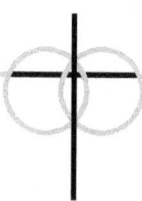

4. *Set a Time Limit:* Set a time frame in which you will make your decision. Don't put important decisions off. Remember: no decision is still a decision.

5. *Accept Mutual Responsibility:* Ask yourselves, How are we as a couple sharing the responsibility for the result of our decision? Is one or are both of us taking on responsibility for this decision?

6. *Reevaluate:* Ask yourselves, Was the decision a life-giving one for us as a couple? Did the decision help or harm our relationship?

Challenges of the Family Life Cycle
Concerning Your Child

- Filling your baby's needs in a loving, caring way that lets your baby feel safe
- Helping your newborn to build trust in you and in the world around him or her
- Helping your toddler gain independence as she or he slowly begins to become aware of herself or himself as a separate, unique individual
- Setting limits with built-in consequences that your child can understand and you can implement
- Providing support and guidance for your child while allowing your child to become increasingly independent
- Teaching your child to communicate feelings as well as thoughts and ideas
- Helping your child deal with the stresses of moving from childhood into adolescence
- Nurturing your child's self-esteem
- Helping your child to complete the last steps of separation and independence while providing love and support

Concerning Your Relationship

- Learning to balance your personal and couple needs with your baby's needs
- Practicing patience with yourselves as you adjust to your new baby
- Working together as parents as you face problems in a way that is most productive for you and your child
- Finding couple time as well as family time
- Sharing responsibilities for the household as well as for childcare
- Setting aside regular times on your calendars for special dates and events for just the two of you
- Keeping couple communication open and sharing your own feelings, thoughts, and ideas
- Being aware of your own goals and needs both as individuals and as a couple
- Developing healthy methods of dealing with the day-to-day stress that this stage of parenting brings
- Standing together in the leadership, guidance, and nurturing of your child
- Nurturing and enjoying yourselves as individuals and as a couple

Spirituality: Bringing It Home

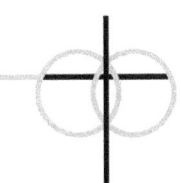

Parallels of Big Church and Little Church

As you enter into the sacrament of Matrimony, you are being called as a married couple to be in union with God and to be aware of his movement in your daily lives. You are also being called to nurture your couple spirituality by being aware that you will be forming your own "Little Church" of the home. This means making God the focal point of your daily lives in living out his faithfulness, love, and fidelity.

It is you, as the People of God, who bring the gift of your "extraordinary" little churches together in community with your parish and the universal Catholic Church. Your home is a sacred place where your love for God, one another, and your family can grow and be nurtured so you can help one another to become saints of ordinary time.

The chart on the right shows how Big Church and Little Church parallel each other.

Big Church   **Little Church**

Liturgy   Family Time/Prayer

Eucharist   Mealtime

Reconciliation   Forgiveness

Sacramentals   Family Treasures

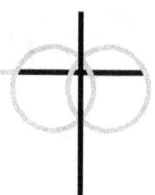

Ideas for Nurturing Couple and Family Spirituality

1. Liturgy/Family Time and Prayer

- Attend Mass weekly, and support your parish with your gifts of time, talent, and financial support.
- Bless one another every morning as you begin the day.
- End each day in prayer by kneeling and thanking God for the gift of one another, naming a special gift your spouse blessed you with that day.
- Take time to build family rituals and celebrate family traditions.
- Make holidays such as Thanksgiving, Christmas, Easter, and even birthdays "holy days" on which God's love is celebrated.

2. Eucharist/Family Meals

- Receive Eucharist, your "bread of life," that feeds and strengthens you on your faith journey.
- Make your dining table a "sacred gathering space" where you pray, eat, share, and feed each other without the interruption of TVs, phones, and other distractions.

- Pray and give thanks to God at meals, even in restaurants and other public places.

3. Reconciliation/Forgiveness

- Make forgiveness and reconciliation a priority in living out God's plan as a married couple. In times of conflict and hurt remember:
  - Saying "I'm sorry" is self-centered. It is about you and how you feel. Asking "Will you forgive me?" is other-centered. It puts your spouse's feelings first. Forgiveness is a two-way action involving both of you.
  - For forgiveness to take place, one person must choose to ask for forgiveness and the other must choose to grant it.
  - The sacrament of Matrimony is a call to unconditional love.

4. Sacramentals/Family Treasures

- Proudly display a crucifix, family bible, statue of the Blessed Virgin Mary, or other holy items as reminders of God's presence in your life.
- Mark your door with a holy sticker or other visible sign so your family and friends are aware that they are entering a Catholic home.

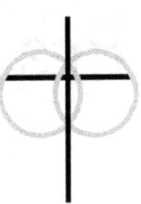

Praying as a Couple

Living a sacramental marriage calls you to live in a more meaningful way. There is a well-known saying: "A family that prays together stays together." In today's world, the power of prayer as a couple and as a family helps keep you focused on God and on your marriage covenant.

Writing a Prayer for Your Spouse

Couple prayer involves sharing your feelings with each other and with God. To do this, reflect on the following:

Dear God,

The special gift with which my spouse has blessed me today is:

_____

_____

_____

_____

The blessing I ask for our Little Church of the home is:

_____

_____

_____

_____

I want to increase our couple spirituality by promising to:

_____

_____

_____

_____

Prayers

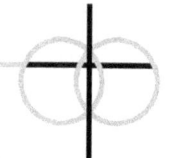

Team Blessing for Convalidation Couples

Team Leaders: Lord, earlier we lit this candle
as a reminder to these couples
that their love for one another
is a sign of God's presence in the world.

They have worked hard
to prepare for the sacrament of Matrimony,
and now we, their team,
ask your blessings upon them as we send them forth.

Be with each of these couples in the days ahead
and help them to grow more deeply in love
with you and with one another.

Be with each of them on their wedding day in the Church,
so that they may truly realize
the power of your presence
and experience the fruits of your sanctifying grace.

Be with each of them
in their upcoming sacramental/sacred marriage
so that they will always feel
your love, support, and sacred presence in their life together.

All: *Amen.*

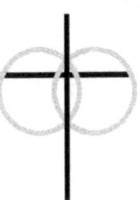

A Couple's Prayer

Lord, as we prepare for the sacrament of Matrimony, help us to stay centered on our love for you and one another. As our convalidation day approaches, give us wisdom to grow in our mutual respect and love for one another. On that day, be with us as we exchange our precious vows. Send us your grace as we become the living promise of the sacrament of Matrimony, so that we will always bring your love to each other and to those whose lives we touch. *Amen.*

A Married Couple's Prayer

Lord, bless us as we live out our sacrament in our day-to-day lives. Give us the strength to keep each other always as our number one priority. Help us to be a reflection of your love to our spouse. Thank you for the great gift of our love. Help us to nurture it with ongoing respect, commitment, and affection for each other. Lord, as our years of marriage increase, may we find that you are the center of our lives. May our love for each other strengthen us as well as be a source of faith and hope to our family and Church community. *Amen.*

A Family Prayer

Loving God, strengthen and protect our loving relationship that we may always enjoy the gift of our marriage to one another. We ask you to watch over our families today and every day, as we struggle to model the Holy Family in our homes. Help us to have the strength to go against the grain of society to reflect your teachings and your Son's example. We ask you to empower us with the wisdom to consistently make the decisions in our lives that will give life to our families and each other. Thank you for the wonderful gift of our family and help us always to reflect your love to them. Bless us, Lord, as we strive to live out our marriage as a strong and loving couple. *Amen.*

Our Family Prayer

Using the format provided here, compose your own prayer, asking God to help you with your unique hopes and fears:

Dear God,

I ask you for...

_____

_____

_____

_____

I am anxious about...

_____

_____

_____

_____

I am grateful for...

_____

_____

_____

_____

Additional Topics

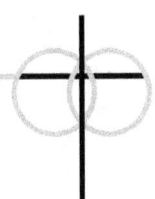

Note: The following topics have been added to help you further prepare for the sacrament of Matrimony. It is important to take time to reflect and talk about the areas that are relevant to your relationship.

Ecumenical and Interfaith Couples

What Are Ecumenical and Interfaith Marriages?

For many years, the Catholic Church has recognized the importance of being open to other religions and sharing the richness of different faith traditions. The primary goal of ecumenism is to foster unity among all Christians so that the one body of Christ may be a visible sign of salvation for all men and women.

Today, an increasing number of Catholic marriages are ecumenical and interfaith marriages. An *ecumenical marriage* is the union between a Catholic and another baptized Christian. An *interfaith marriage* is the union between a Catholic and one who is not of the Christian tradition.

Ecumenical or interfaith marriage can succeed. It is not always easy, but with respect, openness, and strong communication, it is possible. Couples with strong spiritual commitments enjoy fulfilling marriages. The primary concern of the Church is to uphold the strength and stability of the marital union and the family that flows from it, regardless of whether both spouses are Catholic.

Hints for Building a Strong Ecumenical or Interfaith Marriage

You are encouraged as a couple to be sensitive and understanding about the topic of religion. Your varying religious traditions offer the opportunity to share special gifts and unique points of view. Here are some hints that other ecumenical or interfaith couples have found helpful:

- Give each other the right to continue practicing your respective religions. It is vital to understand the importance of religious beliefs and the special need to support each other even if you do not always agree with or understand one another in these matters. Discontinuing your religious practices in the hope of pleasing your spouse or making life simpler is never the answer.
- Communication is vital to the successful sharing of religious traditions and beliefs in ecumenical and interfaith marriages. Strive to learn more about your spouse's religious convictions. Often, you will find areas of agreement and understanding.
- Celebrate your similarities and respect your differences.
- Build a combined family spirituality that includes elements from both faith traditions.
- Listen to each other's feelings about your faith, beliefs, and practices.
- Occasionally, attend each other's religious services and get to know the congregation and ministers. This can be a rewarding and unifying experience and can help you understand more about your spouse's religion, including putting mistaken ideas to rest.

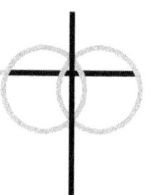

- Take the time to discuss the religious upbringing of your children. Not giving your children any religious training to avoid conflict is unfair to them.
- Speak with other married couples who have ecumenical or interfaith relationships and who are striving for unity. Ask how they have dealt with the challenges and how they share the joys of their respective faiths with each other.
- Participate as a couple in ministry activities within both religious communities. This can strengthen your individual faiths and be a sign of your shared faith.
- Family prayer is an important part of any couple's relationship, and sharing the prayers and rituals of the two faiths can enrich and strengthen the family.

Special Notes for Ecumenical/Interfaith Couples

In ecumenical and interfaith marriages, the Catholic party makes a statement acknowledging the obligation to preserve and protect his or her faith and promises to do everything possible to have the children baptized and brought up in the Catholic Church. The non-Catholic must be informed of the promises and responsibilities of the Catholic.

In preparing your wedding, it is certainly possible to arrange for the minister or rabbi of the party who is not Catholic to take part in the ceremony. This can make the ceremony more comfortable and acceptable to the families of the couple and can be a step in joining the families in a lifelong community.

It is common that an ecumenical or interfaith couple getting married in the Catholic Church decides on a wedding ceremony outside of the Mass called a Liturgy of the Word. This type of liturgical celebration does not include the celebration of the Eucharist or the reception of Holy Communion. Many times, this is more comfortable for family and friends who are not Catholic, since they may not be familiar with the Mass.

Natural Family Planning

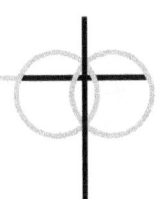

Easy to Learn

Natural Family Planning (NFP) is user friendly. The two basic methods, ovulation and sympto-thermal, can be learned over three menstrual cycles. Couples are taught to observe, record, and interpret the woman's unique signs of fertility as ovulation approaches. They also learn to recognize those signs that tell the women she is no longer fertile in each cycle.

A multinational study found that, irrespective of culture, education, or economic background, over 95% of women can recognize their mucus signs of fertility. Certified teachers provide individual and classroom instruction.

The Gift

One of the most beautiful gifts God has given each of us is our sexuality. How we express our sexuality is determined by the vocation to which God has called us. We are created in the image and likeness of God. No matter what our vocation, we are called to reflect God's love in all relationships. We need only to look to Jesus on the cross to understand authentic love. Jesus loved us so much that He made a complete gift of himself to us, which in turn, is what we are called to do.

In order for a couple to experience the totality of God's intended plan for them, it is necessary for each act of intercourse to be open to life, whether or not it results in pregnancy. Artificial forms of contraception act as a barrier to the transmission of life. Consequently, a couple who uses an artificial form of contraception is holding back the gift of their fertility.

The Church understands that couples may have just reason to postpone pregnancy. NFP respects the dignity of marriage as a sacrament. The fertility awareness that NFP provides allows the couple to work with a woman's body. As a sacrament, marriage needs to be free, total, faithful, and fruitful. Consequently, any method of family planning should respect these four traits. NFP does this and so much more.

What Is Natural Family Planning?

Medical researchers have developed NFP through a comprehensive understanding of human biology, which has allowed it to become accurate and precise. NFP relies on the observation of cervical mucus and charting of specific biological markers that all women experience during their fertile years. With proper instruction, couples learn to identify and interpret these signs in order to determine when they are fertile and when they are infertile. This information allows the couple to use the system to achieve, postpone, or avoid pregnancy, depending on what they have discerned God is calling them to in any particular cycle.

There are different methods of learning NFP. It is simply a matter of personal preference as to which method is right for each couple and contacting a certified teacher to be assured of learning the method accurately.

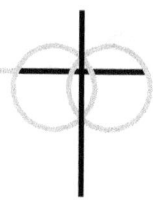

The Benefits of Natural Family Planning

- *99.6% Effective:* NFP is 99.6% effective in postponing pregnancy when used correctly, and it has a 98.4% user effectiveness rate.*
- *100% Natural:* Because NFP is 100% natural, it is 100% safe. There are no harmful risks to the woman's health. It involves no potentially harmful drugs or devices.
- *Low Cost:* NFP is considerably less expensive then birth control. Once instruction is complete, there is no ongoing cost besides chart-related expenses.
- *More Satisfying Marriages:* NFP has proven to have a positive effect on marriage. In times of abstinence, NFP offers couples the opportunity to express affection in other ways, helping to keep their relationship fresh. They also report improved communication and deeper respect for each other.
- *Works with Irregular Cycle:* Women with irregular cycles can still use NFP successfully because the method is based on their personal symptoms of fertility.
- *Helpful for Achieving Pregnancy:* NFP is helpful in achieving pregnancy.

Testimonials for Natural Family Planning

I learned so much about my body in that first class that I vowed never to go back to the pill. I was so amazed to learn about all of the signs that my body would display through my cycle...things that no doctor, no health class, or even my mother ever told me.

—K., New Jersey

When we got married we could have been the poster couple for supposedly needing contraception, [but] I didn't want my wife to put chemicals in her body.

—B., Texas

We are absolutely thrilled with the Sympto-Thermal Method! We finally found peace in planning our family, and I was shocked to find out how much I enjoy not being on the pill anymore. I'm just disappointed that it took so long for us to find that there is an alternative to artificial birth control.

—S., California

Natural Family Planning (NFP) methods are the only forms of family planning that I recommend to my patients because I always want what is best for them. NFP success rates for avoiding pregnancy rival those of contraceptives such as birth control pills. The big difference is that, with NFP, the woman does not ingest hormones or chemicals nor is any device implanted within her. NFP respects the beautiful total giving of one spouse to another that occurs in the marital embrace. The result is that couples who use NFP are happier, healthier, and have very low divorce rates.

—George Delgado, M.D, San Diego, California

---

* Frank-Herrmann, P., Heil, J. Gnoth, C., et al., "The Effectiveness of a Fertility Awareness Based Method to Avoid Pregnancy in Relation to a Couple's Sexual Behaviour during the Fertile Time: A Prospective Longitudinal Study." *Human Reproduction* 22(5): 1310–1319, 2007.

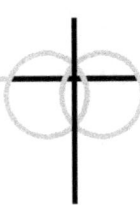

Reflection Questions

1. When I think about using Natural Family Planning, I feel:

___ Excited   ___ Nervous   ___ Unsure

___ Confident   ___ Relieved   ___ Upset

2. Are you open to learning more about Natural Family Planning? Why or why not?

_____

_____

_____

_____

3. If you discussed using another method of family planning, how does it compare to Natural Family Planning with regards to:

Morality:

_____

_____

_____

_____

Relationship:

_____

_____

_____

_____

Effectiveness:

_____

_____

_____

_____

Health benefit:

_____

_____

_____

_____

Resources

- *Plan Your Family Naturally: An Introduction to Natural Family Planning* (DVD), Diocese of Rockville/Office of Faith Formation, drvc-faith.mybigcommerce.com/plan-your-family-naturally
- Billings USA, http://www.boma-usa.org
- International Billings, http://www.woomb.org
- Family of the Americas, http://www.familyplanning.net
- Creighton Model FertilityCare System: http://www.creightonmodel.com, http://www.fertilitycare.org, and http://www.popepaulvi.com
- Symptothermal method: Couple to Couple League, http://www.ccli.org

Your Family/My Family, They're *Our* Family Now!

Marriage joins two families. When you entered into marriage, you were blessed not only by the addition of your new spouse but also by his or her family of origin. Parents, brothers, sisters, aunts, uncles, and sometimes blended families come together as part of your new family. These relatives—yours and your spouse's—all have one thing in common: they love you and want the best for you individually and as a couple.

For you as a convalidation couple, there can be two approaches to the topic of in-laws, depending on how long you have been together:

- How you as a couple relate to your own in-laws
- How you as in-laws relate to your children's spouses

Your In-laws

Each family is a unique blend of personalities, traditions, values, and communication styles. At times, the differences between your families may seem awkward, but the differences can also be a gift that can be embraced. By being open to different approaches to life, you can learn to grow as a family. By combining your family's differences, you can create a wonderfully rich family for your children and/or yourselves as a couple. This is particularly true if you married someone from a different culture. Sharing traditions is an exciting and affirming experience.

Also, you need to keep in mind that no matter how frustrated your spouse may get with his or her own family of origin, he or she still can have a strong sense of attachment and protectiveness toward them. It can be hurtful if you speak badly about or encourage your spouse to speak badly about his or her family. Always remember that your spouse was raised in this family, so they have given you a most treasured gift.

Finally, you need to set a balance in your lives when it comes to spending time with your respective families. Remember, the time spent does not have to be 50/50. It must be balanced according to need. Interacting with each other's family can be a rewarding and growth-filled experience for you as individuals, as a couple, and as a family with children. Your in-laws can be a great source of experience and wisdom; however, tension and stress can develop if you find yourself with no personal time for your own family needs.

Following are some warning signs that there are problems concerning in-laws:

- The opinions and/or feelings of your family of origin take priority over those of your spouse.
- You feel closer to your family than you do to your spouse.
- You have frequent arguments involving the topic of in-laws.
- Either or both of you are feeling uncomfortable with or resentful of the amount of time spent with in-laws

Keeping each other number one needs to be a priority. This leads to a balanced and healthy married life, which will enable you to enjoy your relationship with family and friends.

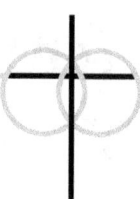

Questions for Reflection about Your In-laws

1. Are you comfortable in your relationship with your in-laws? Why or why not?

2. What are some of the positive qualities and gifts your families bring to you and/or your family?

3. If you have children, how would you describe your in-laws' relationship with them?

4. If you do not have children yet, once they arrive, how would you like their relationship to be with your in-laws?

You as an In-law

As your children become adults and enter into their own marriages, your role grows to include yourself as an in-law. This is an important time to reflect on your experiences with your own in-laws over the years of your relationship. Whether it has been a positive or negative experience, you can learn from it and strive to make your relationship with your married children more enriching.

The same points apply when you become in-laws as applied when you were the son-in-law or daughter-in-law. Being interested in and concerned about your children's lives without overwhelming them is crucial as they begin their married lives. Encourage them to make each other a number one

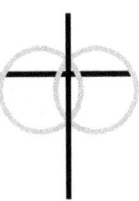

priority and make you their number one fan. A couple who has a loving and encouraging support system from their parents has a much higher rate of success in marriage.

Another challenge for you as a parent is learning to share your son's or daughter's attention with his or her new spouse and family. Parents often complain that their children's in-laws are monopolizing their time, particularly during the holidays. It can be difficult when you feel that you are not able to see your child as often as you would like, particularly when the grandchildren come. Following are some positive ways to be supportive to your children:

- Be understanding when they need time alone or with their in-laws.
- Be open to having combined family celebrations so that everyone's needs can be accommodated and you can all enjoy the time together.
- Encourage your children to celebrate their holidays in their own homes with you visiting them, which can be especially helpful when grandchildren are young.

The main point is that you want to build a supportive and loving relationship with your married children, with their spouses, and their in-laws. If you remember how you wanted to be treated as a daughter-in-law or son-in-law, then you can fashion your attitudes and behavior accordingly and make the relationships reflect your love for your child.

Questions for Reflection about You as In-laws

1. Do you view yourself as a supportive and welcoming in-law? If so, how do you show that to your son-in-law or daughter in-law? If not, how might you improve in this area?

_____

_____

_____

_____

2. Have you had any difficulties in your role as an in-law? How could you lessen these difficulties?

_____

_____

_____

_____

3. Are you happy with your relationship with your grandchildren? If not, how could you improve this relationship?

_____

_____

_____

_____

4. If you do not have grandchildren yet, how are you picturing your role as a grandparent?

_____

_____

_____

_____

QuickWrites

QuickWrites is an activity that your presenters may choose to use throughout the *Picture of Love* program. QuickWrites gives you an opportunity to quickly share and learn additional things about your spouse.

In QuickWrites, you will be asked (individually) to complete statements or answer questions from the following list. As a couple, you'll be asked to share your answers with each other.

You can also use QuickWrites on your own! Pick a statement or question, write down you answers, then take turns sharing how you responded. What have you learned about your spouse?

Statements and Questions

- The most endearing thing you said to me this week was _____.
- You make me smile when you _____.
- My biggest hope for you is _____.
- The reason I love you is _____.
- My favorite place to eat is _____.
- If we could vacation anywhere, I would go _____.
- My favorite movie is _____.
- How much would you spend on a one-time purchase without speaking to your spouse? _____
  _____
- Which holiday did you enjoy the most as a child? _____
- What is your favorite holiday now? _____
- Which of these subjects is the hardest for you to talk about: money, sex, religion, in-laws, or children? _____
- What one thing, that doesn't cost money, does your spouse do for you makes you feel most special?
  _____
- One of the happiest times of my childhood was _____.
- I feel God in my life when I _____.
- I see us using credit throughout our marriage, yes or no? _____.
- One thing I would really like to purchase is _____.
- It is very important that you pray with me, yes or no? _____.

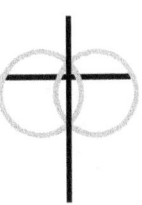

Agree/Disagree

Agree/Disagree is an activity that your presenters may choose to use throughout the *Picture of Love* program. Agree/Disagree gives you an opportunity to share and learn additional things about your spouse.

In the actual activity, you would stand back to back and raise your hand if you agree with the statement and leave your hand down if you disagree. You would then be asked to turn around, revealing your answer to your spouse.

You can also use Agree/Disagree on your own! Pick a statement, write down whether you agree or disagree, then show your response to your spouse. What have you learned about each other?

Statements

On Spirituality

- I feel comfortable praying with you.
- We practice our religion as a couple.
- I want to raise our children in the Catholic faith.
- I want our children to go to Catholic school.

On Family of Origin

- When you marry, you marry the whole family, not just your spouse.
- I am comfortable with our family's Christmas traditions.
- If they ask, we should financially support our families.
- I am comfortable with your family.

On Couple Communication

- I feel comfortable with the amount of time my spouse and I talk together.
- I think that technology gets in the way of our spending time together.
- I feel comfortable communicating with my spouse's family.
- I feel comfortable with how we speak to each other when we are in conflict.

On Finances

- It's okay for me to make a major purchase without consulting you.
- It doesn't matter which one of us makes more money, since it's all ours anyway.
- I am comfortable with our financial situation. I think you spend money well. I think we use debt wisely. We are doing well saving for retirement.

On Intimacy

- I think we are an intimate couple.
- I am worried that when we have children we won't have time for ourselves.
- I am open to hearing about Natural Family Planning.

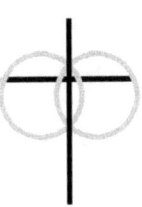

Marriage Preparation Evaluation Form

Date _____   Program Location _____

Please help us evaluate *Picture of Love* by responding to the following:

1. Before the program began, how did you expect it to be?

   _____ Excellent   _____ Good   _____ Fair   _____ Other _____

2. Now, at the end, what is your overall impression of the marriage preparation program?

   _____ Excellent   _____ Good   _____ Fair   _____ Other _____

3. What did you learn that will be most helpful in your marriage?

   _____

   _____

   _____

   _____

4. Is there any topic in particular that you think should be added to the program or expanded upon?

   _____

   _____

   _____

   _____

5. Other comments:

   _____

   _____

   _____

   _____

(continue on next page)

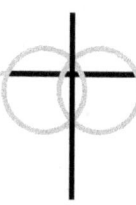

6. If you would like to become a marriage preparation team couple in the future, please provide the following information:

Date of Catholic Marriage: _____

Contact Information:

      Names: _____

      _____

      _____

      Phone number(s): _____

      _____

      Email address(es): _____

      _____

CPSIA information can be obtained
at www.ICGtesting.com
Printed in the USA
JSHW040333270522
26287JS00001B/1